better together*

*This book is best read together, grownup and kid.

 **akidsco.com**

a kids book about

a kids book about being an introvert

by Josh Maynard & Amy Taylor

A Kids Co.
Editor Emma Wolf
Head of Design Rick DeLucco
Publisher Jelani Memory

DK
Editor Emma Roberts
Senior Production Editor Jennifer Murray
Senior Production Controller Louise Minihane
Acquisitions Project Editor Sara Forster
Managing Editor Hazel Eriksson
Publishing Director Mark Searle

First published in Great Britain in 2025 by
Dorling Kindersley Limited
20 Vauxhall Bridge Road,
London SW1V 2SA
A Penguin Random House Company

The authorised representative in the EEA is
Dorling Kindersley Verlag GmbH. Arnulfstr. 124, 80636 Munich, Germany

Text and design copyright © 2025 by A Kids Book About, Inc.
'A Kids Book About' is a trademark of Dorling Kindersley Ltd.
'Kids Are Ready' and the colophon 'a' are trademarks of A Kids Co.
10 9 8 7 6 5 4 3 2 1
002-345792-Nov/2025
All rights reserved.

No part of this publication may be reproduced, stored in or introduced into a retrieval system, or transmitted, in any form, or by any means (electronic, mechanical, photocopying, recording, or otherwise), without the prior written permission of the copyright owner.

No part of this publication may be used or reproduced in any manner for the purpose of training artificial intelligence technologies or systems. In accordance with Article 4(3) of the DSM Directive 2019/790, DK expressly reserves this work from the text and data mining exception.

A CIP catalogue record for this book is available from the British Library.

ISBN: 978-0-2417-2601-3

Printed and bound in China

www.dk.com

akidsco.com

This book was made with Forest Stewardship Council™ certified paper—one small step in DK's commitment to a sustainable future. Learn more at **www.dk.com/uk/information/sustainability**

This book is dedicated to the "quiet kids" (and grownups) of the world.

We see you.
We love you.
We are you.

Intro
for grownups

Ask any grownup introvert and they can probably recall struggling to find their voice and place in the world when they were a kid. There was constant pressure to be sociable, speak up, and be someone different.

That's some serious nonsense.

This book is filled with the message *we* needed once upon a time as introvert kids. Our goal is to validate the experience of introverts and spark important conversations about introversion between little humans and the big humans who love them.

If you're reading this, it's clear you care deeply about the introverted kid in your life. Whether you personally identify as an introvert or not, we hope you'll share your experiences and challenges with your kiddo. And we hope they'll feel seen, safe, and supported knowing that while they may savour their solo time, they're never actually alone in the world. (In our opinion, they're in really great company!)

Have you ever heard someone say...

Why are you so quiet?

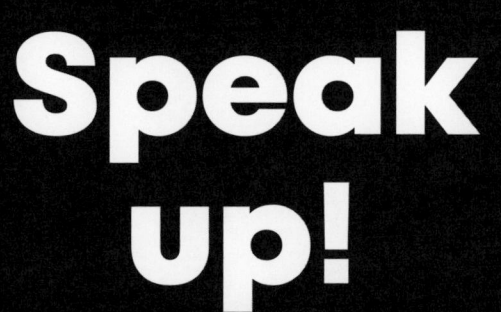

Almost every introvert on the planet has heard these words.

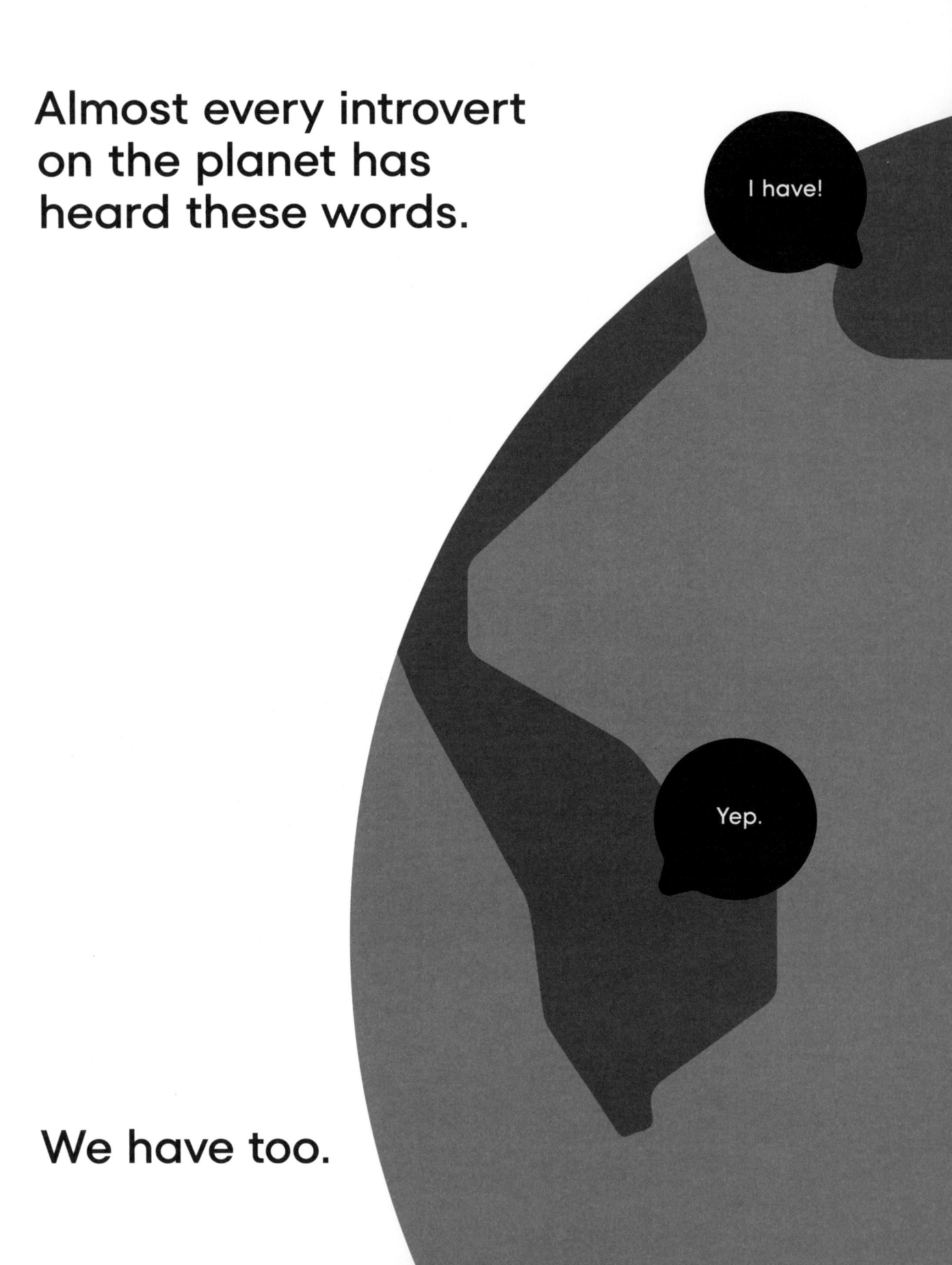

We have too.

Part of growing up means exploring what it means to be...

unique

ely
you.

But these kinds of words can make you doubt yourself, or feel like you need to pretend to be someone you're not.

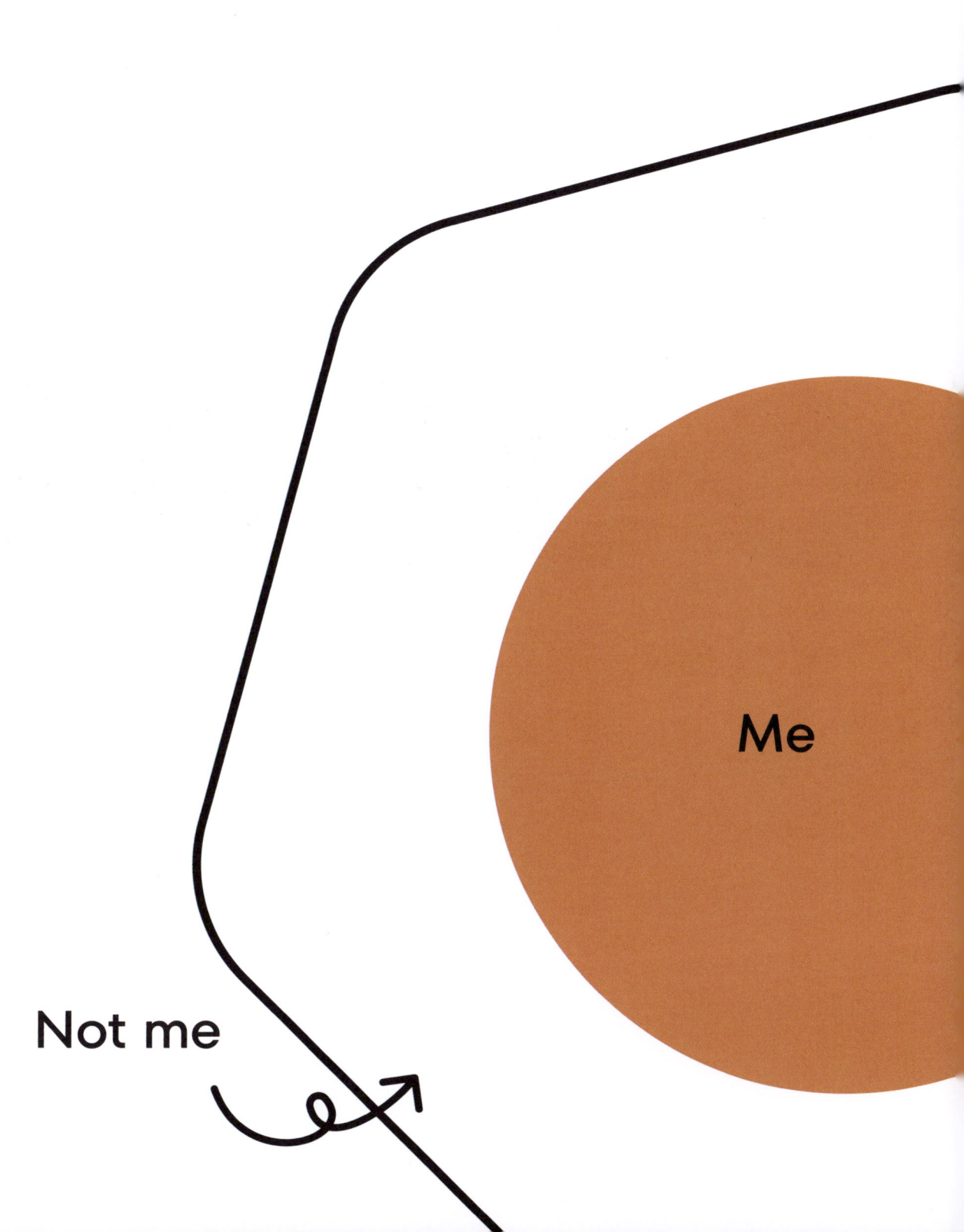

This book is
for introverts,
and exists to

celeb

rate

the "quiet kids" of the world.

Hello! We're Amy and Josh. Both of us are introverts.

I'm Amy!

I'm a writer, storyteller, introvert, and proud dog mum.

PRO TIP: Sometimes it might be easier to express your thoughts and feelings in writing than in chatty conversation. That's lovely! Words can be just as powerful and magical when written as they are when spoken.

I'm Josh!

I'm a dad to 3 tiny humans, a web designer, and an introvert also.

PRO TIP: When I'm feeling uncomfortable at a party or event, I always look for a pet. Nothing calms my nerves quite like spending time with a cute pup!

And there are sooo many others just like us.

So you might be asking yourself...

Am intro

I an vert?

(What even *is* an introvert?)

We could probably fill 101 books explaining what it means to be an introvert. (Like these do!)

- **The Invisible Boy** by Trudy Ludwig, illustrated by Patrice Barton
- **Sometimes Shy** by Julie Bliven, illustrated by Dang Khoa Tran
- **Wallflowers** by MacKenzie Joy
- **KINDergarten** by Vera Ahiyya, illustrated by Joey Chou
- **I Am Quiet: A Story for the Introvert in All of Us** by Andie Powers, illustrated by Betsy Petersen

But to put it as simply as we can...

- **Shy Willow** by Cat Min
- **How to Party Like a Snail** by Naseem Hrab, illustrated by Kelly Collier
- **Gustavo the Shy Ghost** by Flavia Z. Drago
- **A Way with Wild Things** by Larissa Theule, illustrated by Sara Palacios
- **Captain Starfish** by Davina Bell, illustrated by Allison Colpoys

An introvert is someone who tends to enjoy spending time alone and might feel a little bit overwhelmed in crowds or social situations.

And guess what? There are sooo many introverts out there. They've done some pretty cool things too:

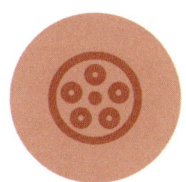 **Iconic actors**
(like Emma Watson)

 **Record-breaking athletes**
(like Lionel Messi)

 **Inspiring world leaders**
(like Barack Obama)

 **Big thinkers**
(like Albert Einstein)

 **Pretty great friends**
(like you!)

Introverts are often called...

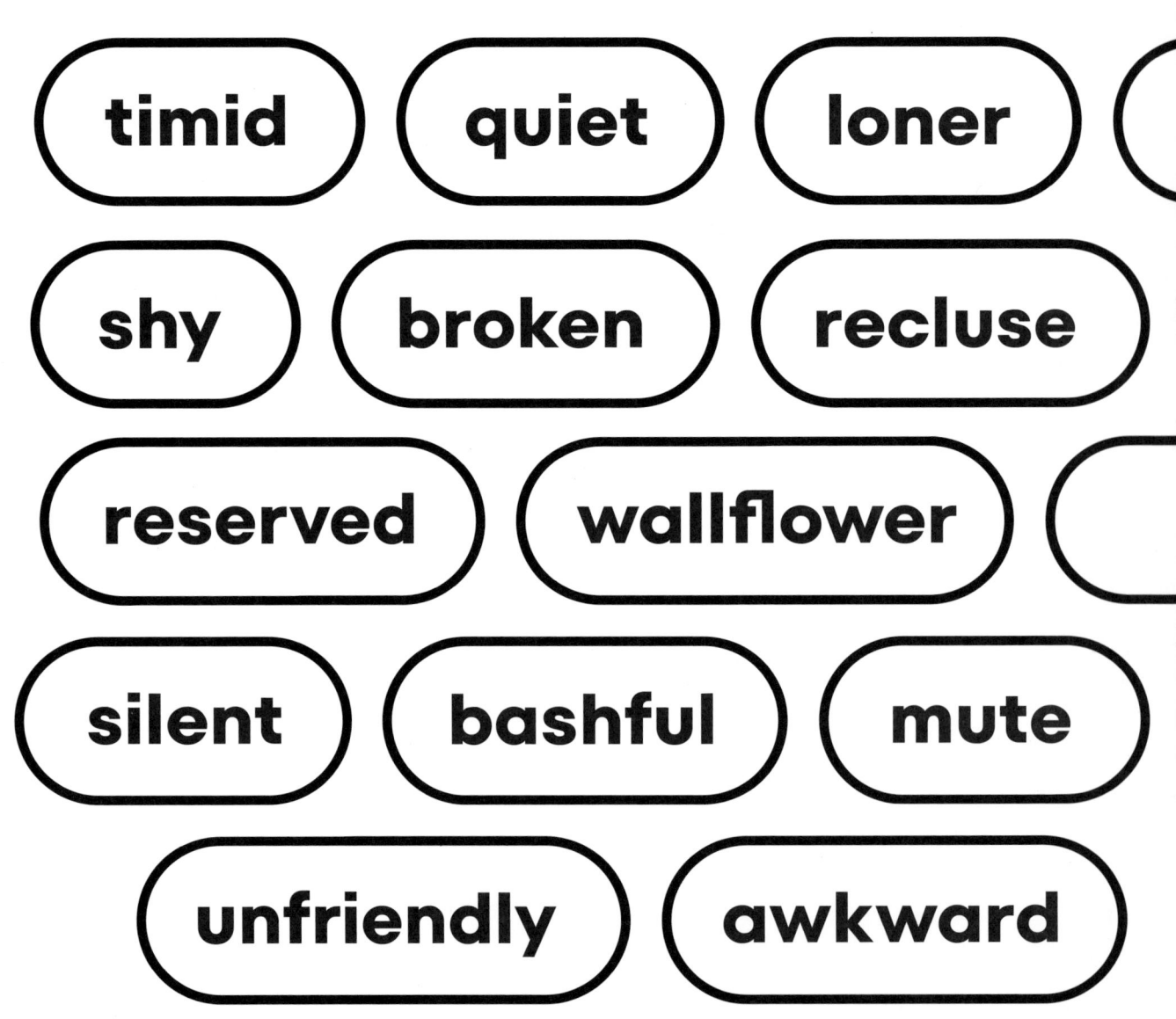

timid quiet loner
shy broken recluse
reserved wallflower
silent bashful mute
unfriendly awkward

anti-social aloof

solitary hermit

detached boring

homebody strange

nerdy or withdrawn.

Have you ever
been called any of
those words?

It may have felt **terrible**.

You may have felt **left out** or **misunderstood**.

These kinds of words can even make us wonder if something is **wrong with us**.

But those words do not make you who you are.

Being an introvert is actually **pretty incredible!**

Take it from us, introverts are...

creative, thoughtful, courageous, and loyal people.

And chances are,
if you're reading
this...

you might be

Hi!

So, what makes an introvert...
an introvert?

Well, introverts are:

1

Good listeners.

We're here for others, especially when they're hurting or struggling.

2

Loyal friends.

We'll stick by the people we care about through thick and thin.

3

Big thinkers.

We're full of creative thoughts and amazing ideas.

4

Really considerate.

We try to think before speaking or acting.

5

Super independent.

We create fun, even when we're on our own.

Other people don't always understand what it's like to be an introvert, though.

Sometimes introverts...

would rather hang out alone than with friends.

need a quiet spot to recharge their batteries.

need extra time to think before answering a question.

take time getting to know someone before being completely comfortable around them.

All of those things are **fine**, **good**, and **normal**.

Every kid is different!

Some kids love performing on stage.

Some kids have lots of friends.

Some kids like answering their teacher's questions in front of the whole class.

But for some kids, it feels scary – even impossible.

Some kids prefer 1 or 2 friends they know really, really well.

And some kids are happiest at home, reading their favourite book.

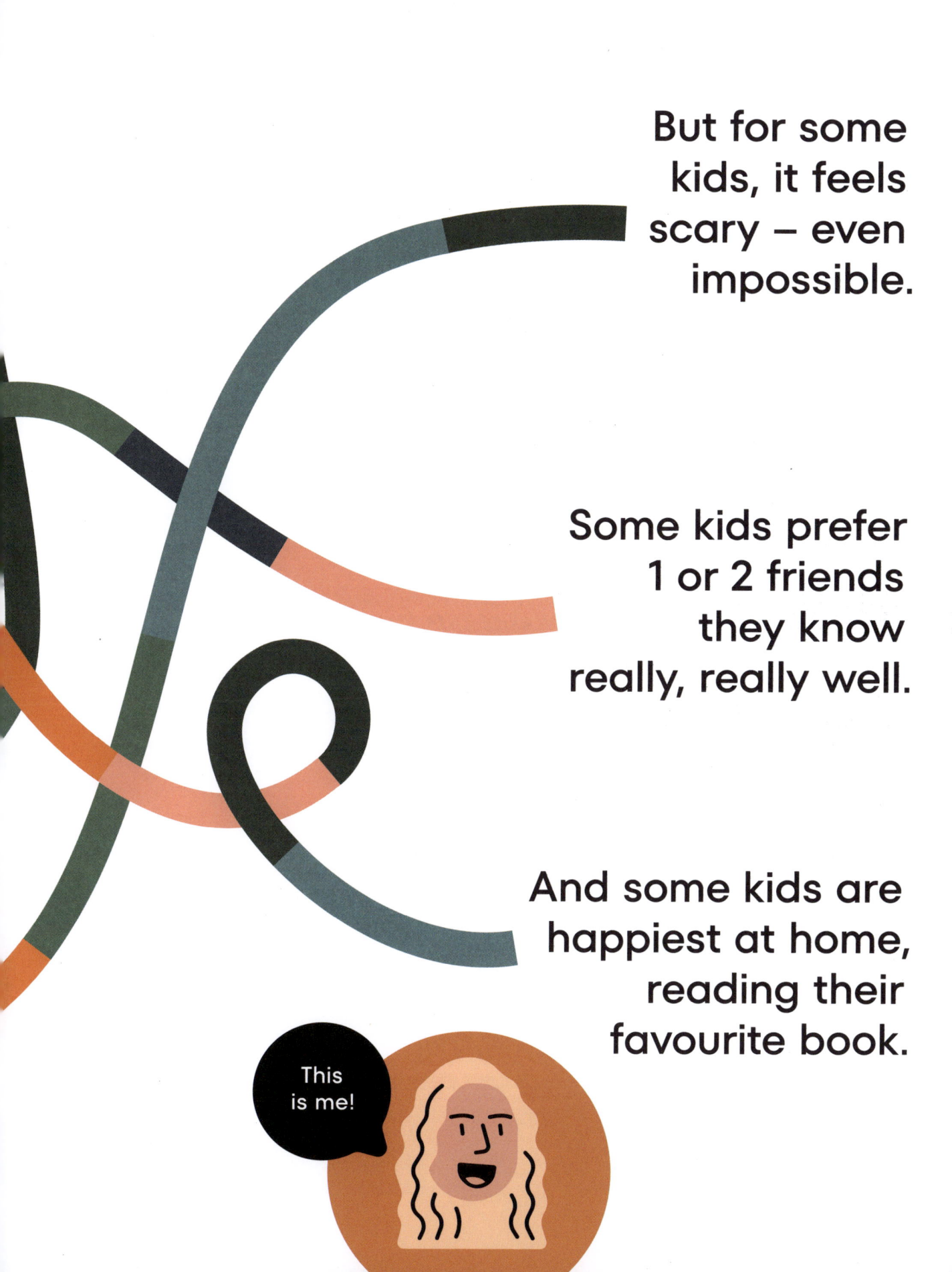

There are so many different ways to be human.

There's no right or wrong.

It's about what makes you feel **safe** and **secure**.

And because each of us is so unique, that can look sooooo different.

introvert

You may be here today.

Or maybe you're here.

And that's OK!

———————— **extrovert**

So if you're a fellow introvert, we've got some important things to tell you.

Listen up!

It's perfectly fine to say no to a sleepover or overnight camp if you don't feel comfortable.

If it feels overwhelming to raise your hand in class, talk to your teachers about other ways of sharing your thoughts – maybe through writing!

You don't need to hang out in a group if you'd rather spend time with a friend one-on-one.

Don't worry about trying to be like everyone else.

Remember — what others may think about you or call you does not make you who you are.

If you feel like you might be an introvert, we think these words are a much more accurate description of all the good things you are...

kind curious patient

intelligent considerate

thoughtful observant

loyal helpful

creative gentle deep

understanding interesting

respectful empathetic

caring and amazing!

By being true to your introverted self, you make the world a...

kinder, better place, where everyone feels safe, accepted, & welcome.

Exactly as
they are.

Outro
for grownups

Hello again, grownups. This book is just the beginning of a much bigger (and very important) conversation about the value of introverts and how we can advocate for the introverts in our lives.

But don't fret! Fostering introvert inclusivity can be as simple as offering alternate ways of doing things to make our introverted kiddos feel seen, safe, and supported, so they can fully shine.

If you notice your kid feeling overwhelmed or overstimulated at a social gathering, help them find a quiet spot to take a breather. If you have students in your class who hesitate to raise their hand, consider integrating a written option for sharing their thoughts. The possibilities are endless. One thing that's certain? They'll never forget what it feels like, knowing you're on their side.

Looking for additional resources? All of the books from the earlier illustration are real!

About The Authors

Josh Maynard (he/him) is a designer in Arvada, Colorado, with a focus on creating more accessible web experiences for all. As a lifelong introvert and a dad to 3 (boisterous) tiny humans, he has the incredible challenge of finding much-needed time to recharge his introvert batteries while managing the ever-present to-do list that comes with dad duty.

Amy Taylor (she/her) is an Ohio-based writer and storyteller. As a kid, she was a certified chatterbox, but that started to feel like wearing socks 3 sizes too small as she aged into adulthood. Today, she's a proud introvert who feels most like herself when spending time with her family, rescue dog, and garden.

Made to empower.

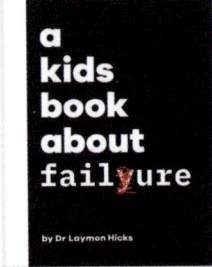   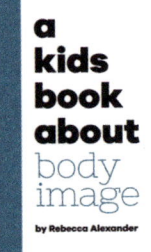 
   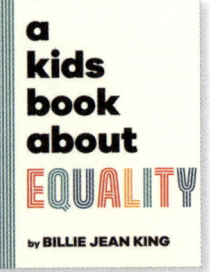 
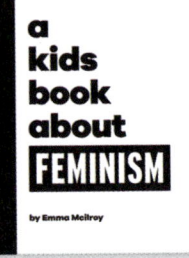    

Discover more at akidsco.com